FLUENCY THEATER
Teacher's Guide
Set 6

Contents

Finally . . . a program that provides engaging fluency instruction for *all* your readers:

Steck-Vaughn Fluency Theater

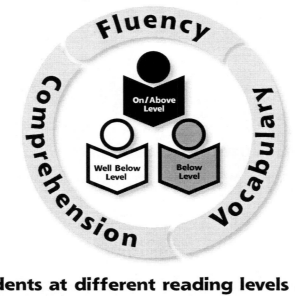

Students at different reading levels . . .
Practicing the *same* selections
Pursuing the *same* instructional goals
Interacting and building fluency *together!*

Students build fluency through a reader's theater play and three connected readings.

The **play** has 6 character roles at three different reading levels:

 Well Below Level

Below Level

On/Above Level

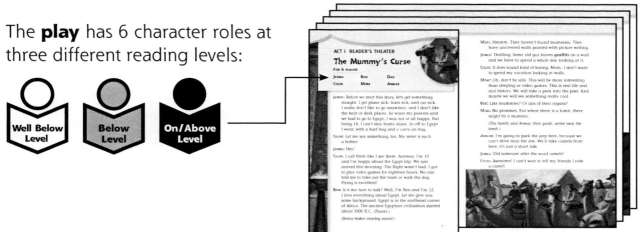

ACT I READER'S THEATER
The Mummy's Curse
FOR 6 PLAYERS

| JENNA | BEN | DAD |
| COLIN | MOM | ANWAR |

JENNA: Before we start this story, let's get something straight. I get plane sick, train sick, and car sick. I really don't like to go anywhere, and I don't like the heat or dark places. So when my parents said we had to go to Egypt, I was not at all happy. But being 14, I can't stay home alone. So off to Egypt I went, with a barf bag and a carry-on bag.

COLIN: Let me say something, too. My sister is such a bother.

JENNA: Hey!

COLIN: I call them like I see them. Anyway, I'm 10 and I'm happy about the Egypt trip. We just arrived this morning. The flight wasn't bad. I got to play video games for eighteen hours. No one told me to take out the trash or walk the dog. Flying is excellent!

BEN: Is it my turn to talk? Well, I'm Ben and I'm 12. I love everything about Egypt. Let me give you some background. Egypt is in the northeast corner of Africa. The ancient Egyptian civilization started about 3000 B.C. (Pauses.)

(Jenna makes snoring sound.)

MOM: Hmmm. They haven't found mummies. They have uncovered walls pointed with picture writing.

JENNA: Thrilling. Some old guy leaves graffiti on a wall and we have to spend a whole day looking at it.

COLIN: It does sound kind of boring, Mom. I don't want to spend my vacation looking at walls.

MOM: Oh, don't be silly. This will be more interesting than sleeping or video games. This is real life and real history. We will take a peek into the past. And maybe we will see something really cool.

BEN: Like mummies? Or jars of their organs?

MOM: No promises. But where there is a tomb, there might be a mummy.

(The family and Anwar, their guide, arrive near the tomb.)

ANWAR: I'm going to park the jeep here, because we can't drive near the site. We'll take camels from here; it's just a short ride.

JENNA: Did someone utter the word camels?

COLIN: Awesome! I can't wait to tell my friends I rode a camel!

Each fiction or nonfiction **connected reading** is at one of three levels:

 Well Below Level

Below Level

On/Above Level

ACT II CONNECTED READINGS
Mummies

Mummies aren't just something from creepy science fiction movies. They are real people who died. They wanted their bodies kept in good condition. They believed they needed their bodies for life after death.

Ancient Egyptians learned ways to keep the bodies of the dead in good condition. Here is how the Egyptians made mummies. First they removed all the organs from the dead body. They put the organs in jars. Then they covered the body in salt. They let it dry for one month. They wrapped the body in linen. They put charms and jewels in the layers of linen. They wrapped the body in a sheet. They placed the Book of the Dead in the sheet. Last they coated the sheet with wax and perfume.

Today X-rays can show a mummy's skeleton. They can also show objects buried with the mummy. X-rays can help scientists answer questions about mummies.

FLUENCY TIP
To practice phrasing, rewrite the first paragraph. Draw a slash mark (/) after each phrase. For example: "In the past/ scientists unwrapped mummies/ to study them."

17

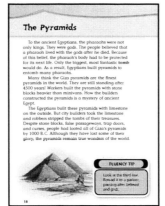

The Pyramids

To the ancient Egyptians, the pharaohs were not only kings. They were gods. The people believed that a pharaoh lived with the gods after he died. Because of this belief, the pharaoh's body had to be protected for its next life. Only the biggest, most fantastic tomb would do. As a result, Egyptians built pyramids to entomb many pharaohs.

Many think the Giza pyramids are the finest pyramids in the world. They are still standing after 4500 years! Workers built the pyramids with stone blocks heavier than minivans. How the builders constructed the pyramids is a mystery of ancient Egypt.

The Egyptians built these pyramids with limestone on the outside. But city builders took the limestone and robbers stripped the tombs of their treasures. Despite stone blocks, false passageways, trap doors, and curses, people had looted all of Giza's pyramids by 1000 B.C. Although they have lost some of their glory, the pyramids remain true wonders of the world.

FLUENCY TIP
Look at the third line. Reread it to a partner, pausing after tombs and gods.

18

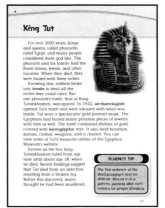

King Tut

For over 3000 years, kings and queens called pharaohs ruled Egypt, and many people considered them god-like. The pharaoh and his family had the finest linens, jewels, and other luxuries. When they died, their riches went with them.

Knowing this, robbers broke into tombs to steal all the riches they could carry. But one pharaoh's tomb, that of King Tutankhamen, was spared. In 1922, archaeologists opened Tut's tomb and were amazed with what was inside. Tut was a spectacular gold portrait mask. The Egyptians had buried many priceless pieces of jewelry with him as well. The tomb contained shrines of gold, covered with hieroglyphic text. It also held furniture, statues, clothes, weapons, and a chariot. You can view some of Tut's treasures online at the Egyptian Museum's website.

Known as the boy king, Tutankhamen ruled from age nine until about age 18, when he died. Recent findings suggest that Tut died from an infection resulting from a broken leg. Before this discovery, many thought he had been murdered.

FLUENCY TIP
The first sentence of the third paragraph may be difficult. Reread it to a partner, pausing after each comma for proper phrasing.

19

Fluency Theater's simple design helps you put the spotlight on reading success!

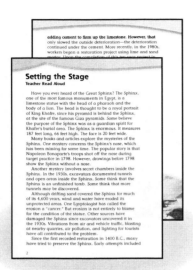

1. Teacher Read Aloud

Introduce the book's topics or themes while modeling good fluency.

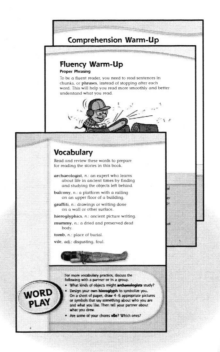

2. Instructional Warm-Ups

Provide focused pre-reading instruction that includes vocabulary exploration and strategies for fluency and comprehension.

3. Reader's Theater Play

Move into the play, encouraging student groups to interact, discuss, and build fluency as they read and re-read their leveled lines.

6. Curtain Call

Check comprehension, assign engaging extension activities, and then . . . take a bow!

5. Connected Readings

Continue fluency building with fiction or non-fiction selections that relate to the play.

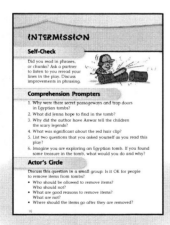

4. Intermission

Pause to check comprehension and to allow students to extend the play's ideas through discussion or writing.

The Fluency Theater Lesson Plan . . .
A clear, structured approach to fluency building

The key to developing fluency is **practice.** Each Fluency Theater Teacher's Guide lesson provides that practice through a routine of five instructionally focused rehearsals.

1. **First Rehearsal**

2. **Vocabulary Rehearsal**

3. **Fluency Rehearsal**

4. **Comprehension Rehearsal**

5. **Final Rehearsal**

Lesson Plan

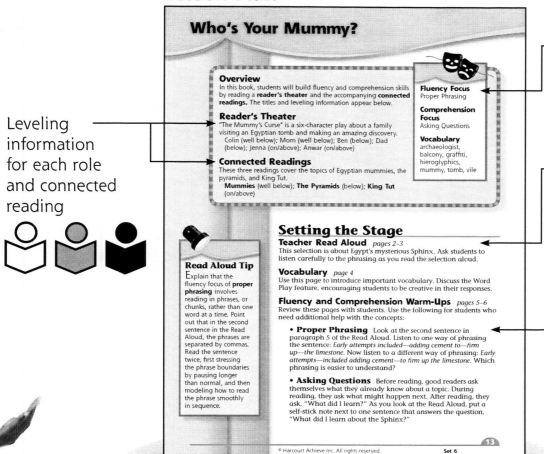

Who's Your Mummy?

Overview
In this book, students will build fluency and comprehension skills by reading a **reader's theater** and the accompanying **connected readings.** The titles and leveling information appear below.

Reader's Theater
"The Mummy's Curse" is a six-character play about a family visiting an Egyptian tomb and making an amazing discovery. Colin (well below); Mom (well below); Ben (below); Dad (below); Jenna (on/above); Anwar (on/above)

Connected Readings
These three readings cover the topics of Egyptian mummies, the pyramids, and King Tut.
Mummies (well below); **The Pyramids** (below); **King Tut** (on/above)

Fluency Focus
Proper Phrasing

Comprehension Focus
Asking Questions

Vocabulary
archaeologist, balcony, graffiti, hieroglyphics, mummy, tomb, vile

Setting the Stage

Teacher Read Aloud *pages 2–3*
This selection is about Egypt's mysterious Sphinx. Ask students to listen carefully to the phrasing as you read the selection aloud.

Vocabulary *page 4*
Use this page to introduce important vocabulary. Discuss the Word Play feature, encouraging students to be creative in their responses.

Fluency and Comprehension Warm-Ups *pages 5–6*
Review these pages with students. Use the following for students who need additional help with the concepts:

• **Proper Phrasing** Look at the second sentence in paragraph 5 of the Read Aloud. Listen to one way of phrasing the sentence: *Early attempts included—adding cement to—firm up—the limestone.* Now listen to a different way of phrasing: *Early attempts—included adding cement—to firm up the limestone.* Which phrasing is easier to understand?

• **Asking Questions** Before reading, good readers ask themselves what they already know about a topic. During reading, they ask what might happen next. After reading, they ask, "What did I learn?" As you look at the Read Aloud, put a self-stick note next to one sentence that answers the question, "What did I learn about the Sphinx?"

Read Aloud Tip
Explain that the fluency focus of **proper phrasing** involves reading in phrases, or chunks, rather than one word at a time. Point out that in the second sentence in the Read Aloud, the phrases are separated by commas. Read the sentence twice, first stressing the phrase boundaries by pausing longer than normal, and then modeling how to read the phrase smoothly in sequence.

Set 6 13

(annotations surrounding the lesson plan)

Leveling information for each role and connected reading

Listing of the lesson's instructional focuses and key vocabulary

Overview of the Read Aloud along with tips for modeling fluency and introducing the lesson's fluency focus

Ideas for supporting the student book's explanation of the lesson's instructional focuses

---

Relevant student pages . . .

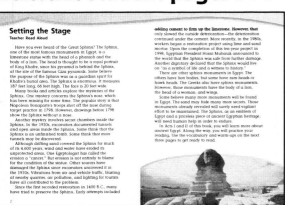

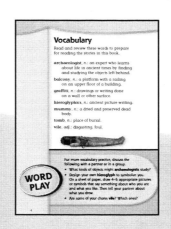

Opportunity for students to build confidence before beginning group work

Tip for engaging student groups in another meaningful vocabulary activity

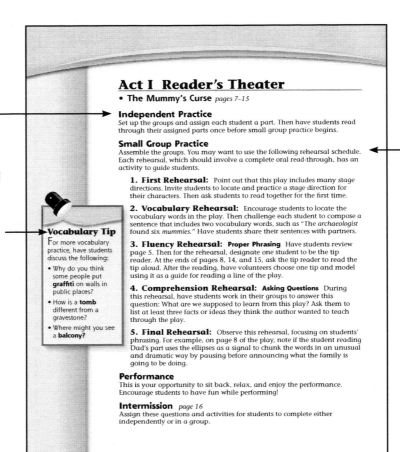

Act I Reader's Theater
• **The Mummy's Curse** *pages 7–15*

Independent Practice
Set up the groups and assign each student a part. Then have students read through their assigned parts once before small group practice begins.

Small Group Practice
Assemble the groups. You may want to use the following rehearsal schedule. Each rehearsal, which should involve a complete oral read-through, has an activity to guide students.

1. First Rehearsal: Point out that this play includes many stage directions. Invite students to locate and practice a stage direction for their characters. Then ask students to read together for the first time.

2. Vocabulary Rehearsal: Encourage students to locate the vocabulary words in the play. Then challenge each student to compose a sentence that includes two vocabulary words, such as "The *archaeologist* found six *mummies*." Have students share their sentences with partners.

3. Fluency Rehearsal: Proper Phrasing Have students review page 5. Then for the rehearsal, designate one student to be the tip reader. At the ends of pages 8, 14, and 15, ask the tip reader to read the tip aloud. After the reading, have volunteers choose one tip and model using it as a guide for reading a line of the play.

4. Comprehension Rehearsal: Asking Questions During this rehearsal, have students work in their groups to answer this question: What are we supposed to learn from this play? Ask them to list at least three facts or ideas they think the author wanted to teach through the play.

5. Final Rehearsal: Observe this rehearsal, focusing on students' phrasing. For example, on page 8 of the play, note if the student reading Dad's part uses the ellipses as a signal to chunk the words in an unusual and dramatic way by pausing before announcing what the family is going to be doing.

Performance
This is your opportunity to sit back, relax, and enjoy the performance. Encourage students to have fun while performing!

Intermission *page 16*
Assign these questions and activities for students to complete either independently or in a group.

Vocabulary Tip
For more vocabulary practice, have students discuss the following:
• Why do you think some people put **graffiti** on walls in public places?
• How is a **tomb** different from a gravestone?
• Where might you see a **balcony**?

14

Routine of five rehearsals, the heart of the lesson. The routine breaks the complex process of oral reading into simple, manageable activities, **each with its own instructional focus.**

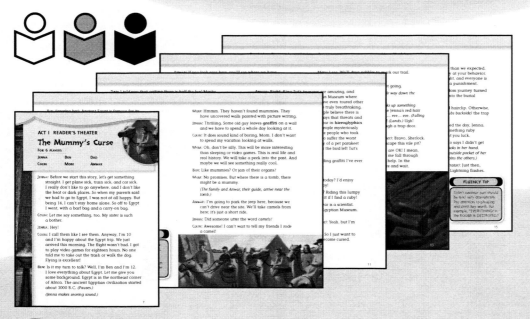

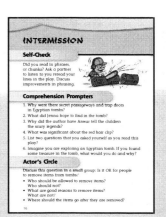

Act II Connected Readings
- **Mummies** (well below) *page 17* • **The Pyramids** (below) *page 18*
- **King Tut** (on/above) *page 19*

Independent Practice
Break each Act I group into two: one group of three (with 1 well below level, 1 below, 1 on/above) and another group of three (1 well below, 1 below, 1 on/above). Assign each member a different selection based on level. Then have students read through their selections once.

Small Group Practice
Assemble the groups. As with the play rehearsals, each rehearsal in the schedule below has an activity to guide students.

1. First Rehearsal: Guide students to preview their selections by reading the titles and looking at the accompanying illustration or photograph. Ask each student to predict one thing he or she might learn from the selection. Then ask students to read their selections aloud to the group.

2. Vocabulary Rehearsal: Before this rehearsal, ask each student to choose a vocabulary word from his or her selection. Have students think of a question that includes the word, such as "Why did the Egyptians make mummies?" Have students work in their groups to ask and answer their questions.

3. Fluency Rehearsal: Proper Phrasing Have students review the fluency instruction on page 5 and the tips in their selections. After the reading, have each student choose one sentence and copy it twice. Challenge students to mark the sentences to show different phrasing. Then invite them to read both sentences to partners and to work with their partners to decide which sentence sounds better.

4. Comprehension Rehearsal: Asking Questions Review the questions at the bottom of page 6. Have each student choose one question to ask about his or her selection. Challenge other students to write the questions and answers. Invite students to share their questions and answers by reading them aloud to the group.

5. Final Rehearsal: Observe each student's reading. Give last-minute pointers for the performance to come, modeling the pointers as appropriate.

Performance
As with the performance of the play, enjoy the reading!

Curtain Call *page 20*
Have groups answer the relevant Comprehension Prompter questions. For the Taking It Further activity, you may want to form new groups.

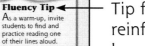

Fluency Tip
As a warm-up, invite students to find and practice reading one of their lines aloud. Encourage students to use punctuation as a guide to proper phrasing by pausing when they come to commas and stopping when they come to periods.

Tip for reinforcing the lesson's fluency focus with a simple activity

15

Set 6

ACT II CONNECTED READINGS

Mummies

Mummies aren't just something from creepy science fiction movies. They are real people who died. They wanted their bodies kept in good condition. They believed they needed their bodies for life after death.

Ancient Egyptians learned ways to keep the bodies of the dead in good condition. Here is how the Egyptians made mummies. First they removed all the organs from the dead body. They put the organs in jars. Then they covered the body in salt. They let it dry for one month. They wrapped the body in linen. They put charms and jewels in the layers of linen. They wrapped the body in a sheet. They placed the Book of the Dead in the sheet. Last they coated the sheet with wax and perfume.

Today X-rays can show a mummy's skeleton. They can also show objects buried with the mummy. X-rays can help scientists answer questions about mummies.

FLUENCY TIP

To practice phrasing, reread the first paragraph. Draw a slash mark (/) after each phrase. For example: "It's the part/ I will/ is unwrapped/ mysteries/ to study them."

17

The Pyramids

To the ancient Egyptians, the pharaohs were not only kings. They were gods. The people believed that a pharaoh lived with the gods after he died. Because of this belief, the pharaoh's body had to be protected for its next life. Only the biggest, most fantastic **tomb** would do. As a result, Egyptians built pyramids to entomb many pharaohs.

Many think the Giza pyramids are the finest pyramids in the world. They are still standing after 4500 years! Workers built the pyramids with stone blocks heavier than minivans. How the builders constructed the pyramids is a mystery of ancient Egypt.

The Egyptians built these pyramids with limestone on the outside. But city builders took the limestone and robbers stripped the tombs of their treasures. Despite stone blocks, false passageways, trap doors, and curses, people had looted all of Giza's pyramids by 1000 B.C. Although they have lost some of their glory, the pyramids remain true wonders of the world.

FLUENCY TIP

Look at the first line. Reread it to a partner, pausing after "Egyptians" and "gods."

18

King Tut

For over 3000 years, kings and queens called pharaohs ruled Egypt, and many people considered them god-like. The pharaoh and his family had the finest linens, jewels, and other luxuries. When they died, they were buried with these riches.

Knowing this, robbers broke into **tombs** to steal all the riches they could carry. But one pharaoh's tomb, that of King Tutankhamen, was spared. In 1922, **archaeologists** opened Tut's tomb and were amazed with what was inside. Tut wore a spectacular gold portrait mask. The Egyptians had buried many priceless pieces of jewelry with him as well. The tomb contained shrines of gold, covered with **hieroglyphic** text. It also held furniture, statues, clothes, weapons, and a chariot. You can view some of Tut's treasures online at the Egyptian Museum's website.

Known as the boy king, Tutankhamen ruled from age nine until about age 18, when he died. Recent findings suggest that Tut died from an infection resulting from a broken leg. Before this discovery, many thought he had been murdered.

FLUENCY TIP

The first sentence of the third paragraph may be difficult. Reread it to a partner, pausing after each comma for proper phrasing.

19

CURTAIN CALL

Reread
Reread your assigned Act II article several more times aloud. Remember to chunk the text into phrases that sound natural and smooth. The more you practice your reading, the better reader you will become!

Comprehension Prompters
1. Mummies
   A. What supplies do you need to wrap a mummy properly for burial?
   B. Do you think people should be mummified? Tell why or why not.

2. The Pyramids
   A. How did tomb builders try to prevent robberies?
   B. What especially puzzles us about how the Egyptians built the pyramids?

3. King Tut
   A. What was found in King Tut's tomb?
   B. Name two unusual things about King Tut and his tomb.

Taking It Further
What was school like in ancient Egypt? At age 11 or 12, would you be in school if you lived back then? Or would you be expected or forced to do something else?
- Research education in ancient Egypt.
- Find out who went to school and for how many years.
- Make a Venn diagram comparing schools of ancient Egypt to schools today.

20

Blackline master assessing vocabulary, comprehension, and fluency

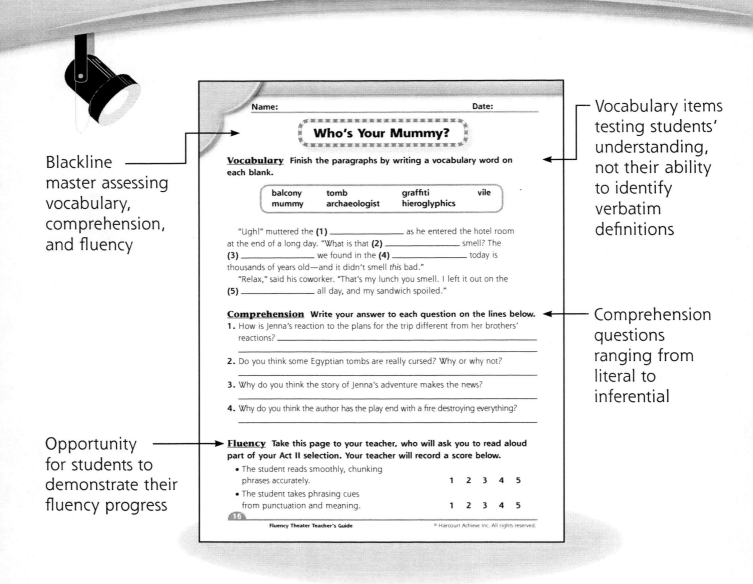

Name: _____ **Date:** _____

Who's Your Mummy?

Vocabulary Finish the paragraphs by writing a vocabulary word on each blank.

balcony	tomb	graffiti	vile
mummy	archaeologist	hieroglyphics	

"Ugh!" muttered the **(1)** _____ as he entered the hotel room at the end of a long day. "What is that **(2)** _____ smell? The **(3)** _____ we found in the **(4)** _____ today is thousands of years old—and it didn't smell *this* bad."

"Relax," said his coworker. "That's my lunch you smell. I left it out on the **(5)** _____ all day, and my sandwich spoiled."

Comprehension Write your answer to each question on the lines below.

1. How is Jenna's reaction to the plans for the trip different from her brothers' reactions? _____

2. Do you think some Egyptian tombs are really cursed? Why or why not? _____

3. Why do you think the story of Jenna's adventure makes the news? _____

4. Why do you think the author has the play end with a fire destroying everything? _____

Fluency Take this page to your teacher, who will ask you to read aloud part of your Act II selection. Your teacher will record a score below.

- The student reads smoothly, chunking phrases accurately. 1 2 3 4 5
- The student takes phrasing cues from punctuation and meaning. 1 2 3 4 5

16

Fluency Theater Teacher's Guide

Vocabulary items testing students' understanding, not their ability to identify verbatim definitions

Comprehension questions ranging from literal to inferential

Opportunity for students to demonstrate their fluency progress

The **Fluency Theater** Lesson Plan . . . Systematic fluency support from beginning to end—all in just four pages!

Leveling and Grouping

The instructional power of the **small mixed-0ability group** is at the heart of Steck-Vaughn Fluency Theater. Each student book and lesson plan has been carefully built to promote meaningful group interaction. In contrast to independent reading, young readers using Fluency Theater build skills in a rich environment of peer-to-peer modeling, discussion, and feedback.

Leveling Information

Act I: Reader's Theater

The play has **6 roles** at 3 different reading levels. The level of each role is indicated by color in the student book:

 blue role green role red role

Act II: Connected Readings

There are **3 connected readings**, each at one of 3 reading levels. The level of each reading is indicated by the order in which it appears in the book:

 first selection second selection third selection

Grouping Recommendations

Act I: Reader's Theater

Set up groups of 6 students, assigning each student a role according to reading level.

Act II: Connected Readings

Break each Act I group into 2 groups of 3, as recommended in each lesson. Assign each student a selection according to reading level.

A Final Note

The leveling indicators are a guide, not a rule. As an experienced classroom teacher, you may want to use additional factors—such as class size or student interest—in deciding how to assign roles and form groups. For example, in order to make the group numbers work for the size of your class, you may choose to assign an on-level student a below-level role. Be assured that an on-level student reading a below-level role will still benefit from meaningful interaction with the group.

The Power of Reader's Theater
by Jo Worthy

Of all the approaches I have used in 28 years of working with adolescents, reader's theater is the most loved among students and teachers. Fortunately, there are many reasons why reader's theater is also an excellent use of instructional time.

Reader's Theater Improves Fluency

Fluent reading is important because comprehension—the goal of reading—depends on it. In repeated reading, the most common form of fluency instruction, students read a text segment two or more times, attempting to read faster and with fewer mistakes each time.

Unfortunately, students often get bored with repeated reading because it's not something a person would do in real life. Reader's theater gives students an authentic reason to engage in repeated reading. When students practice to perform reader's theater, they know they will be performing for an audience, so they read their scripts over and over until they can read them accurately and quickly.

Reader's Theater Grabs All Readers

There's something about "hiding behind a script" that grabs the interest of even the shiest, most resistant reader. Take Juan, for example, one of the most reserved boys I have ever met. When I interviewed him about his experiences with reader's theater, he said he at first felt "really scared." In his first few roles, he did not want to read by himself. However, gradually, he began to look forward to performances and to having his own role.

Reader's Theater Is an Engaging Way to Address All Aspects of Reading

Interpreting a script for an audience requires students to be active meaning makers. They need to read with appropriate speed and expression so the audience will understand and enjoy the performance. Because they know they will be performing for an audience—even if it's just their own classmates—students take it seriously.

Reader's theater is the only approach I have used in which every student—even the ones who claim to hate to read—will read on their own time.

Jo Worthy

It's Greek to Me!

Overview
In this book, students will build fluency and comprehension skills by reading a **reader's theater** and the accompanying **connected readings.** The titles and leveling information appear below.

Reader's Theater
"Eros and Psyche" is a six-character play that retells the Greek myth in which Eros, the god of love, upsets his mother by falling in love with Psyche.

Eros (well below); Psyche's Sister (well below); Narrator 1 (below); Psyche (below); Narrator 2 (on/above); Aphrodite (on/above)

Connected Readings
These three readings are adaptations of fables first told centuries ago by Aesop.

The Boy Who Cried Wolf (well below); **The Crow and the Snake** (below); **The Man and the Lion** (on/above)

Fluency Focus
Proper Phrasing

Comprehension Focus
Monitoring Comprehension

Vocabulary
arrogance, deceiving, destiny, innocent, maiden, mortal, troth, vanity/vain

Read Aloud Tip

Explain that the fluency focus of **proper phrasing** involves reading in chunks, rather than one word at a time. Punctuation is often a clue as to how to chunk a sentence. Point out that in the last sentence under the heading *Comedy* in the Read Aloud, the dashes are clues as to how to chunk the sentence. Read the sentence twice, first without pausing and next by pausing at the dashes.

Setting the Stage

Teacher Read Aloud *pages 2–3*
This selection is about Greek influences on theater and on the two types of plays—tragedies and comedies. As you read aloud, model using proper phrasing by reading in meaningful chunks.

Vocabulary *page 4*
Use this page to introduce important vocabulary. Discuss the Word Play feature, reminding students to use the supplied definitions to help with their responses.

Fluency and Comprehension Warm-Ups *pages 5–6*
Review these pages with students. Use the following for students who need additional help with the concepts:

- **Proper Phrasing** Think about the meaning of what you read. Remember to chunk words into phrases that make sense. For example, in the first sentence under the heading *Tragedy,* it makes sense to chunk the words *Unlike a comedy,—a tragedy—explores human suffering.* Chunks like *Unlike a comedy, a—tragedy explores human—suffering* don't make sense.

- **Monitoring Comprehension** When you monitor your reading, you ask yourself whether you understand the words and ideas. If you come to an unfamiliar word, you stop to figure it out. Look at the word *scheming* in the paragraph under *Comedy.* Find the word in a dictionary and read the meaning.

1

Set 6

Act I Reader's Theater

- **Eros and Psyche** *pages 7–15*

Independent Practice

Set up the groups and assign each student a part. Then have students read through their assigned parts once before small group practice begins.

Small Group Practice

Assemble the groups. You may want to use the following rehearsal schedule. Each rehearsal, which should involve a complete oral read-through, has an activity to guide students.

1. First Rehearsal: Allow students to preview the play by reading the title and the list of characters. Assist with the pronunciation of character names if needed. Students will then read together as a group for the first time.

2. Vocabulary Rehearsal: Before this rehearsal, ask each student to illustrate one of the play's vocabulary words. Give students time to share their illustrations with their groups, and invite volunteers to guess the word being represented.

3. Fluency Rehearsal: Proper Phrasing Review the fluency instruction on page 5. Ask students to choose one of their lines that includes a comma. Have students read their lines aloud, emphasizing the phrasing, and then ask other group members to echo-read each sentence.

4. Comprehension Rehearsal: Monitoring Comprehension Before this rehearsal, have each student skim the text and use self-stick notes to mark at least two words that are not vocabulary words but that are unusual or difficult words. Have them find these selected words in a dictionary. Provide time for students to share the words and definitions in their groups.

5. Final Rehearsal: Observe this rehearsal, focusing on students' phrasing. For example, have students read in unison Psyche's lines that begin at the top of page 13, exaggerating pauses when they reach a comma or period.

Performance

This is your opportunity to sit back, relax, and enjoy the performance. Encourage students to have fun while performing!

Intermission *page 16*

Assign these questions and activities for students to complete either independently or in a group.

Vocabulary Tip

For more vocabulary practice, have students discuss the following:

- What does it mean to be "**innocent** until proven guilty"?
- What behaviors would you expect to see from a character who is **vain?**
- Have you ever read a book or seen a movie about a young **maiden?** If so, what was it?

Act II Connected Readings

- **The Boy Who Cried Wolf** (well below) *page 17*
- **The Crow and the Snake** (below) *page 18*
- **The Man and the Lion** (on/above) *page 19*

Independent Practice
Break each Act I group into two: one group of three (with 1 well below level, 1 below, 1 on/above) and another group of three (1 well below, 1 below, 1 on/above). Assign each member a different selection based on level. Then have students read through their selections once.

Small Group Practice
Assemble the groups. As with the play rehearsals, each rehearsal in the schedule below has an activity to guide students.

1. First Rehearsal: Allow students time to preview their selections by reading the titles and studying the illustrations. Afterward, have students read their selections aloud to the group.

2. Vocabulary Rehearsal: Ask students to locate any selection vocabulary words. Have each student choose one word and read aloud the sentence that includes the word.

3. Fluency Rehearsal: Proper Phrasing Before this rehearsal begins, ask students to locate and read the Fluency Tip for their selection. After the rehearsal, ask students to model using their tips as they read aloud the appropriate text.

4. Comprehension Rehearsal: Monitoring Comprehension After this rehearsal, have students look for context clues for the word listed below from their selection. Have them explain how the context clues helped them understand their words.

- *The Boy Who Cried Wolf:* liar (Lesson)
- *The Crow and the Snake:* brimming (paragraph 1)
- *The Man and the Lion:* prowess (paragraph 1)

5. Final Rehearsal: Observe each student's reading. Give last-minute pointers for the performance to come, modeling the pointers as appropriate.

Performance
As with the performance of the play, enjoy the reading!

Curtain Call *page 20*
Have groups answer the relevant Comprehension Prompter questions. For the Taking It Further activity, you may want to form new groups.

Fluency Tip
Write a sentence from one selection on the board. Model reading the sentence in chunks. Then draw lines to show how you broke the sentence into phrases. Have each student choose a sentence from his or her selection to read in meaningful chunks to a partner.

It's Greek to Me!

Vocabulary Write the vocabulary word that answers each question.

> destiny   mortal   deceiving   troth
> maiden   arrogance   innocent   vanity

1. Which word means the opposite of *guilty*? _____
2. Which word means "what becomes of a person or thing"? _____
3. Which word is a synonym for *tricking*? _____
4. Which word can be used to describe both an animal and a human being?
   _____
5. Which word is a synonym for *young woman*? _____

Comprehension Write your answer to each question on the lines below.

1. How does Aphrodite's dislike for Psyche lead to war on the earth? _____
   _____

2. Why does Eros hide his identity from his bride? _____
   _____

3. Do you think Eros is right to send Psyche away for looking at him? Why or
   why not? _____
   _____

4. Imagine that you could become immortal. What is one problem living forever
   might cause for you? _____
   _____

Fluency Take this page to your teacher, who will ask you to read aloud
part of your Act II selection. Your teacher will record a score below.

- The student reads smoothly, chunking
  phrases accurately.   1   2   3   4   5
- The student takes phrasing cues
  from punctuation and meaning.   1   2   3   4   5

From the Inside Out

Overview
In this book, students will build fluency and comprehension skills by reading a **reader's theater** and the accompanying **connected readings.** The titles and leveling information appear below.

Reader's Theater
"Who Calls the Shots?" is a six-character play about a boy who has a strange daydream due to his worries about being too short.
Daniel (well below); Mom (well below); Theo Thyroid (below); Ali Adrenal (below); Pete Pituitary (on/above); Dr. Mendoza (on/above)

Connected Readings
These three readings cover the topics of the brain, nervous system, and digestive system.
Your Brain (well below); **Your Nervous System** (below); **Your Digestive System** (on/above)

Fluency Focus
Reading with Word Accuracy

Comprehension Focus
Building Background

Vocabulary
bloodstream, genes, heredity, hormones, metabolism, network, unique

Read Aloud Tip
Introduce the fluency focus of **reading with word accuracy.** Write *contraction* and *simultaneously* on the board. Point out that good readers think about how to pronounce difficult words. They look at each part of the word and then put the parts together. Have students read each word with you, first stressing the separate syllables and then reading the whole word aloud.

Setting the Stage

Teacher Read Aloud *pages 2–3*
This selection is about the heart and how it works. Read the selection aloud, modeling good fluency by pronouncing each word clearly and accurately.

Vocabulary *page 4*
Use this page to introduce important vocabulary. Discuss the Word Play feature, encouraging students to be creative in their responses.

Fluency and Comprehension Warm-Ups *pages 5–6*
Review these pages with students. Use the following for students who need additional help with the concepts:

- **Reading with Word Accuracy** When you come to an unfamiliar word, remember to look for parts of the word that you know. Put the parts together to say a word that makes sense. Then practice saying the word. Try doing this with words from the Read Aloud, such as *nutrients* and *digested.*

- **Building Background** Thinking about what you already know about a topic helps you understand what you read. List at least three things you already know about the heart or the bloodstream. Underline one fact that helps you understand what the Read Aloud is about. What reference books and Internet resources could you use to find more information?

Set 6

Act I Reader's Theater

- **Who Calls the Shots?** *pages 7–15*

Independent Practice

Set up the groups and assign each student a part. Then have students read through their assigned parts once before small group practice begins.

Small Group Practice

Assemble the groups. You may want to use the following rehearsal schedule. Each rehearsal, which should involve a complete oral read-through, has an activity to guide students.

1. First Rehearsal: Students will read together as a group for the first time. Remind them to preview the play for difficult words to practice ahead of time and to re-read sentences that don't make sense.

2. Vocabulary Rehearsal: Before this rehearsal, have students locate and list the vocabulary words used in the play. Ask group members to turn back to page 4 and alternate reading aloud the definitions for the listed words.

3. Fluency Rehearsal: Reading with Word Accuracy Draw students' attention to the word *enlighten* on page 9 of the play. Point out that the word is made up of a prefix (*en-*), a root word (*light*), and a suffix (*-en*). Model pronouncing the prefix, root, and suffix and then blending them together. Have students locate and read aloud additional words with prefixes or suffixes on page 9. (*mighty, bigger, located, divided, produces, longer, thicker*)

4. Comprehension Rehearsal: Building Background After this rehearsal, have students work in groups to create T-Charts to record what they know about the endocrine system and what they want to find out.

5. Final Rehearsal: Observe this rehearsal, focusing on students' ability to read with word accuracy. For example, does the student reading the part of Ali Adrenal pronounce the prefix, root, and suffix in the word *triangular* on page 12?

Performance

This is your opportunity to sit back, relax, and enjoy the performance. Encourage students to have fun while performing!

Intermission *page 16*

Assign these questions and activities for students to complete either independently or in a group.

Vocabulary Tip

What characteristics do you possess that are probably due to **heredity?**

- What might be the result of the body not producing enough growth **hormone?**

- How does what you eat relate to your **bloodstream?**

Act II Connected Readings

- **Your Brain** (well below) *page 17*
- **Your Nervous System** (below) *page 18*
- **Your Digestive System** (on/above) *page 19*

Independent Practice
Break each Act I group into two: one group of three (with 1 well below level, 1 below, 1 on/above) and another group of three (1 well below, 1 below, 1 on/above). Assign each member a different selection based on level. Then have students read through their selections once.

Small Group Practice
Assemble the groups. As with the play rehearsals, each rehearsal in the schedule below has an activity to guide students.

1. First Rehearsal: Guide students to preview their selections by scanning them for difficult words to practice ahead of time. Then have students read their selections aloud to the group.

2. Vocabulary Rehearsal: Before this rehearsal, ask students to locate any selection vocabulary words. Encourage them to look at page 4 to review the meanings of the words used in their selections. Then have each student read aloud the sentence that includes the word.

3. Fluency Rehearsal: Reading with Word Accuracy Before the rehearsal, challenge each student to choose one or two long or unfamiliar words from his or her selection and read each word aloud twice. The first time, they should stretch the word out to say the individual parts: *chem—i—cals.* The second time, they should blend the parts to say the word naturally: *chemicals.*

4. Comprehension Rehearsal: Building Background After the rehearsal, ask students to think of one or two questions they have about the body system featured in their selections. Have students record their questions on large index cards. Later, provide reference materials so that students can learn more about the systems. Invite students to write answers to their questions on the backs of the cards.

5. Final Rehearsal: Observe each student's reading. Give last-minute pointers for the performance to come, modeling the pointers as appropriate.

Fluency Tip
Before students do their first read-through of the selections, model reading science-related words by looking for word parts and blending them. For example, the word parts *re—cep—tors* blend to form the word *receptors.*

Performance
As with the performance of the play, enjoy the reading!

Curtain Call *page 20*
Have groups answer the relevant Comprehension Prompter questions. For the Taking It Further activity, you may want to form new groups.

Set 6

From the Inside Out

Vocabulary Write the number of a vocabulary word on the blank before its meaning.

1. heredity
2. network
3. unique
4. genes
5. metabolism
6. hormones
7. bloodstream

_____ Group of things working together as a system

_____ Substances that control heredity

_____ System of blood flowing though the body

_____ Passing of physical characteristics from parents to children

_____ One-of-a-kind

_____ Process of chemical change that provides energy for the body

_____ Substances that affect the body's growth and development

Comprehension Write your answer to each question on the lines below.

1. What is Daniel concerned about at the beginning of the play? _____
_____

2. Which character refers to himself as captain of the endocrine "team"? _____
_____

3. What is the endocrine system and what does it do? _____
_____

4. What did Daniel learn about his own growth and development? _____
_____

Fluency Take this page to your teacher, who will ask you to read aloud part of your Act II selection. Your teacher will record a score below.

- The student reads all words accurately.   1 2 3 4 5
- The student blends together letters that make one sound.   1 2 3 4 5

Fluency Theater Teacher's Guide

Secrets in Stone

Overview
In this book, students will build fluency and comprehension skills by reading a **reader's theater** and the accompanying **connected readings.** The titles and leveling information appear below.

Reader's Theater
"The Writing Is on the Wall" is a six-character play about a class field trip to the Museum of Archaeology.
  Selena (well below); Andre (well below); Miss Williams (below); Jeremy (below); Colette (on/above); Museum Guide (on/above)

Connected Readings
These three readings describe several important archaeological discoveries: Easter Island, the Rosetta Stone, and Stonehenge.
  Easter Island (well below); **Rosetta Stone** (below); **Stonehenge** (on/above)

Fluency Focus
Using Expression

Comprehension Focus
Determining the Main Idea

Vocabulary
archaeologist, decipher, epigrapher, geologist, hieroglyphics, paleontologist, replica, scribe

Read Aloud Tip

Introduce the fluency focus of **using expression.** Explain that readers make text more interesting by stressing key words. Re-read the last sentence in paragraph 1 of the Read Aloud, emphasizing the words *Hittites, Maya,* and *Aztec.* Invite students to suggest a word to stress in the next paragraph, and then have a volunteer read that sentence aloud.

Setting the Stage

Teacher Read Aloud   *pages 2–3*
This selection is about ancient hieroglyphic writing and the different peoples that used it. Ask students to listen carefully to your expression as you read the selection aloud.

Vocabulary   *page 4*
Use this page to introduce important vocabulary. Discuss the Word Play feature, encouraging students to use specific, concrete details in their responses.

Fluency and Comprehension Warm-Ups   *pages 5–6*
Review these pages with students. Use the following for students who need additional help with the concepts:

- **Using Expression** Part of reading with expression is deciding what words to stress, or read with a stronger voice. Read the first sentence of the Read Aloud together, stressing these important words: *writing, ideas, sounds.*

- **Determining the Main Idea** An entire selection has a main idea. Often, so does each paragraph within the selection. Look at paragraph 6 of the Read Aloud. Find and read aloud the sentence that describes the main idea.

9

Set 6

Act I Reader's Theater

- **The Writing Is on the Wall** *pages 7–15*

Independent Practice
Set up the groups and assign each student a part. Then have students read through their assigned parts once before small group practice begins.

Small Group Practice
Assemble the groups. You may want to use the following rehearsal schedule. Each rehearsal, which should involve a complete oral read-through, has an activity to guide students.

1. First Rehearsal: Invite students to scan the entire play to find italicized stage directions. Point out that these directions tell actors how to speak or what to do. Then ask students to read together as a group for the first time.

2. Vocabulary Rehearsal: Have students locate the vocabulary words used in the play. As students locate each word, ask them to read in unison the sentence that includes that word. Challenge volunteers to use the words in sentences that explain the words' meaning, such as: "An *archaeologist* is a person who studies ancient cultures."

3. Fluency Rehearsal: Using Expression Review page 5 and the Fluency Tips on pages 8, 11, and 14. Remind students to consider the characters' feelings and to use their voices to express them. After the reading, ask students to work in groups to locate two or three sentences that express excitement or other feelings and to take turns reading them to the group.

4. Comprehension Rehearsal: Determining the Main Idea After this rehearsal, have students work in their groups to create Idea Webs. The Idea Web should list the main idea of the play in the center and at least six details in smaller circles around the main idea.

5. Final Rehearsal: Observe this rehearsal, focusing on students' expression. For example, for Jeremy's first lines on page 7, note whether the student raises his or her voice at the end of the first sentence and uses an excited tone of voice for the second sentence.

Performance
This is your opportunity to sit back, relax, and enjoy the performance. Encourage students to have fun while performing!

Intermission *page 16*
Assign these questions and activities for students to complete either independently or in a group.

Vocabulary Tip

For more vocabulary practice, have students discuss the following:

- How does the work of an **archaeologist** differ from that of a **geologist?**

- Who would be more interested in dinosaurs: an **epigrapher** or a **paleontologist?**

Act II Connected Readings

- **Easter Island** (well below) *page 17*
- **Rosetta Stone** (below) *page 18*
- **Stonehenge** (on/above) *page 19*

Independent Practice
Break each Act I group into two: one group of three (with 1 well below level, 1 below, 1 on/above) and another group of three (1 well below, 1 below, 1 on/above). Assign each member a different selection based on level. Then have students read through their selections once.

Small Group Practice
Assemble the groups. As with the play rehearsals, each rehearsal in the schedule below has an activity to guide students.

1. First Rehearsal: Ask students to read the titles of their selections aloud. Have students discuss what they already know about the topics. Also suggest that each student review any photograph that accompanies the selection. Then have each student read the selection aloud to the group.

2. Vocabulary Rehearsal: Ask students to locate any selection vocabulary words. Invite students to alternate reading aloud their words and to identify which word appears in two of the selections. *(archaeologists)*

3. Fluency Rehearsal: Using Expression Before this rehearsal, encourage students to read the Fluency Tips for their selections. After the rehearsal, have each student write one sentence from his or her selection on a sheet of paper. Challenge students to underline the words that should be stressed. Invite them to take turns reading the sentences aloud in their groups, stressing the underlined words.

4. Comprehension Rehearsal: Determining the Main Idea Before this rehearsal, review the comprehension instruction on page 6. After the rehearsal, ask each student to write the main idea of his or her selection in two sentences or fewer. Invite students to read their main idea sentences aloud in their groups.

5. Final Rehearsal: Observe each student's reading. Give last-minute pointers for the performance to come, modeling the pointers as appropriate.

Fluency Tip
As a warm-up, invite students to find and practice reading aloud a line from their selection that includes either a comma or an exclamation point.

Performance
As with the performance of the play, enjoy the reading!

Curtain Call *page 20*
Have groups answer the relevant Comprehension Prompter questions. For the Taking It Further activity, you may want to form new groups.

Set 6

Secrets in Stone

Vocabulary Write each vocabulary word on the blank where it belongs.

epigrapher	paleontologist	decipher	scribe
replica	archaeologist	geologist	hieroglyphics

1. His writing was so sloppy that it was almost impossible to _____!

2. The author of this book about volcanoes is a(n) _____.

3. My brother is building a(n) _____ of an Egyptian pyramid.

4. A(n) _____ discovered a rare fossil.

5. The walls of the tomb are covered with _____.

Comprehension Write your answer to each question on the lines below.

1. What is one reason ancient people carved pictures into stone? _____
_____

2. Why do you think the museum has replicas of the stones found on Easter Island instead of the actual stones? _____
_____

3. Why is it easier to decipher hieroglyphics today than it was during the 1800s?
_____
_____

4. Would you rather work as an epigrapher or an archaeologist? Why?
_____
_____

Fluency Take this page to your teacher, who will ask you to read aloud part of your Act II selection. Your teacher will record a score below.

- The student varies voice to enhance meaning.   **1   2   3   4   5**
- The student takes cues from punctuation
  for how to read the sentence.   **1   2   3   4   5**

Fluency Theater Teacher's Guide   © Harcourt Achieve Inc. All rights reserved.

Who's Your Mummy?

Overview
In this book, students will build fluency and comprehension skills by reading a **reader's theater** and the accompanying **connected readings.** The titles and leveling information appear below.

Reader's Theater
"The Mummy's Curse" is a six-character play about a family visiting an Egyptian tomb and making an amazing discovery.
Colin (well below); Mom (well below); Ben (below); Dad (below); Jenna (on/above); Anwar (on/above)

Connected Readings
These three readings cover the topics of Egyptian mummies, the pyramids, and King Tut.
Mummies (well below); **The Pyramids** (below); **King Tut** (on/above)

Fluency Focus
Proper Phrasing

Comprehension Focus
Asking Questions

Vocabulary
archaeologist, balcony, graffiti, hieroglyphics, mummy, tomb, vile

Read Aloud Tip
Explain that the fluency focus of **proper phrasing** involves reading in phrases, or chunks, rather than one word at a time. Point out that in the second sentence in the Read Aloud, the phrases are separated by commas. Read the sentence twice, first stressing the phrase boundaries by pausing longer than normal, and then modeling how to read the phrase smoothly in sequence.

Setting the Stage

Teacher Read Aloud *pages 2–3*
This selection is about Egypt's mysterious Sphinx. Ask students to listen carefully to the phrasing as you read the selection aloud.

Vocabulary *page 4*
Use this page to introduce important vocabulary. Discuss the Word Play feature, encouraging students to be creative in their responses.

Fluency and Comprehension Warm-Ups *pages 5–6*
Review these pages with students. Use the following for students who need additional help with the concepts:

- **Proper Phrasing** Look at the second sentence in paragraph 5 of the Read Aloud. Listen to one way of phrasing the sentence: *Early attempts included—adding cement to—firm up—the limestone.* Now listen to a different way of phrasing: *Early attempts—included adding cement—to firm up the limestone.* Which phrasing is easier to understand?

- **Asking Questions** Before reading, good readers ask themselves what they already know about a topic. During reading, they ask what might happen next. After reading, they ask, "What did I learn?" As you look at the Read Aloud, put a self-stick note next to one sentence that answers the question, "What did I learn about the Sphinx?"

13

Set 6

Act I Reader's Theater

- **The Mummy's Curse** *pages 7–15*

Independent Practice
Set up the groups and assign each student a part. Then have students read through their assigned parts once before small group practice begins.

Small Group Practice
Assemble the groups. You may want to use the following rehearsal schedule. Each rehearsal, which should involve a complete oral read-through, has an activity to guide students.

1. First Rehearsal: Point out that this play includes many stage directions. Invite students to locate and practice a stage direction for their characters. Then ask students to read together for the first time.

2. Vocabulary Rehearsal: Encourage students to locate the vocabulary words in the play. Then challenge each student to compose a sentence that includes two vocabulary words, such as "The *archaeologist* found six *mummies*." Have students share their sentences with partners.

3. Fluency Rehearsal: Proper Phrasing Have students review page 5. Then for the rehearsal, designate one student to be the tip reader. At the ends of pages 8, 14, and 15, ask the tip reader to read the tip aloud. After the reading, have volunteers choose one tip and model using it as a guide for reading a line of the play.

4. Comprehension Rehearsal: Asking Questions During this rehearsal, have students work in their groups to answer this question: What are we supposed to learn from this play? Ask them to list at least three facts or ideas they think the author wanted to teach through the play.

5. Final Rehearsal: Observe this rehearsal, focusing on students' phrasing. For example, on page 8 of the play, note if the student reading Dad's part uses the ellipses as a signal to chunk the words in an unusual and dramatic way by pausing before announcing what the family is going to be doing.

Performance
This is your opportunity to sit back, relax, and enjoy the performance. Encourage students to have fun while performing!

Intermission *page 16*
Assign these questions and activities for students to complete either independently or in a group.

Vocabulary Tip
For more vocabulary practice, have students discuss the following:

- Why do you think some people put **graffiti** on walls in public places?

- How is a **tomb** different from a gravestone?

- Where might you see a **balcony?**

Act II Connected Readings

- **Mummies** (well below) *page 17* • **The Pyramids** (below) *page 18*
- **King Tut** (on/above) *page 19*

Independent Practice

Break each Act I group into two: one group of three (with 1 well below level, 1 below, 1 on/above) and another group of three (1 well below, 1 below, 1 on/above). Assign each member a different selection based on level. Then have students read through their selections once.

Small Group Practice

Assemble the groups. As with the play rehearsals, each rehearsal in the schedule below has an activity to guide students.

1. First Rehearsal: Guide students to preview their selections by reading the titles and looking at the accompanying illustration or photograph. Ask each student to predict one thing he or she might learn from the selection. Then ask students to read their selections aloud to the group.

2. Vocabulary Rehearsal: Before this rehearsal, ask each student to choose a vocabulary word from his or her selection. Have students think of a question that includes the word, such as "Why did the Egyptians make mummies?" Have students work in their groups to ask and answer their questions.

3. Fluency Rehearsal: **Proper Phrasing** Have students review the fluency instruction on page 5 and the tips in their selections. After the reading, have each student choose one sentence and copy it twice. Challenge students to mark the sentences to show different phrasing. Then invite them to read both sentences to partners and to work with their partners to decide which sentence sounds better.

4. Comprehension Rehearsal: **Asking Questions** Review the questions at the bottom of page 6. Have each student choose one question to ask about his or her selection. Challenge other students to write the questions and answers. Invite students to share their questions and answers by reading them aloud to the group.

5. Final Rehearsal: Observe each student's reading. Give last-minute pointers for the performance to come, modeling the pointers as appropriate.

Performance

As with the performance of the play, enjoy the reading!

Curtain Call *page 20*

Have groups answer the relevant Comprehension Prompter questions. For the Taking It Further activity, you may want to form new groups.

Fluency Tip

As a warm-up, invite students to find and practice reading one of their lines aloud. Encourage students to use punctuation as a guide to proper phrasing by pausing when they come to commas and stopping when they come to periods.

15

Set 6

Who's Your Mummy?

Vocabulary Finish the paragraphs by writing a vocabulary word on each blank.

balcony	tomb	graffiti	vile
mummy	archaeologist	hieroglyphics	

"Ugh!" muttered the **(1)** _____ as he entered the hotel room at the end of a long day. "What is that **(2)** _____ smell? The **(3)** _____ we found in the **(4)** _____ today is thousands of years old—and it didn't smell *this* bad."

"Relax," said his coworker. "That's my lunch you smell. I left it out on the **(5)** _____ all day, and my sandwich spoiled."

Comprehension Write your answer to each question on the lines below.

1. How is Jenna's reaction to the plans for the trip different from her brothers' reactions? _____
_____

2. Do you think some Egyptian tombs are really cursed? Why or why not?
_____

3. Why do you think the story of Jenna's adventure makes the news?
_____

4. Why do you think the author has the play end with a fire destroying everything?
_____

Fluency Take this page to your teacher, who will ask you to read aloud part of your Act II selection. Your teacher will record a score below.

- The student reads smoothly, chunking phrases accurately.   1   2   3   4   5
- The student takes phrasing cues from punctuation and meaning.   1   2   3   4   5

Fluency Theater Teacher's Guide

Change Is Good

Overview
In this book, students will build fluency and comprehension skills by reading a **reader's theater** and the accompanying **connected readings.** The titles and leveling information appear below.

Reader's Theater
"Adaptations in Africa" is a six-character play about family members who compare what they learned about animals at the zoo and in Africa.

Uncle Mark (well below); Aunt Trish (well below); Alex (below); Nina (below); Mom (on/above); Dad (on/above)

Connected Readings
These three readings cover the topics of how the arctic fox, anteater, and polar bear have adapted to their habitats.

The Arctic Fox (well below); **The Anteater** (below); **The Polar Bear** (on/above)

Fluency Focus
Using Expression

Comprehension Focus
Making Inferences

Vocabulary
adapt/adaptation, camouflage, gland, habitat, prey, species

Read Aloud Tip
Read the selection once, and then introduce the fluency focus, **using expression.** Ask students to close their eyes and listen to the tone and rhythm of your words as you re-read several paragraphs smoothly and expressively.

Setting the Stage

Teacher Read Aloud *pages 2–3*
This selection is about how animals have adapted to their surroundings. Ask students to listen carefully as you read the selection aloud.

Vocabulary *page 4*
Use this page to introduce important vocabulary. Discuss the Word Play feature, encouraging students to use concrete details in their responses.

Fluency and Comprehension Warm-Ups *pages 5–6*
Review these pages with students. Use the following for students who need additional help with the concepts:

- **Using Expression** Part of reading with expression is deciding what words to stress, or read with a stronger voice. Read the first sentence of the Read Aloud, stressing these important words: *many, animals, lot, water.*

- **Making Inferences** When you make inferences, you use what you read and what you already know to figure things out. What do you know about swimming and diving that helps you infer that whales have huge lungs?

Set 6

Act I Reader's Theater

- **Adaptations in Africa** *pages 7–15*

Independent Practice

Set up the groups and assign each student a part. Then have students read through their assigned parts once before small group practice begins.

Small Group Practice

Assemble the groups. You may want to use the following rehearsal schedule. Each rehearsal, which should involve a complete oral read-through, has an activity to guide students.

> **1. First Rehearsal:** Ask students to preview the play by reading the title, character list, and stage directions. Students should then read the play together as a group for the first time.
>
> **2. Vocabulary Rehearsal:** Have students locate the vocabulary words used in the play and write each word on a separate index card. Then have students take turns choosing a card, reading the word aloud, and using the word in a sentence.
>
> **3. Fluency Rehearsal: Using Expression** Before the rehearsal begins, invite students to review the Fluency Tips by alternating reading them aloud. Then encourage students to have fun by overacting— exaggerating characters' feelings.
>
> **4. Comprehension Rehearsal: Making Inferences** After reading, suggest that students discuss these questions:
>
> > - From what you learned about adaptations, do you think the giraffes thousands of years ago were exactly like the giraffes today? Why or why not?
> > - What do you think the author wants you to learn from this play?
>
> **5. Final Rehearsal:** Observe this rehearsal, focusing on students' expression. For example, when a student reads Dad's first lines on page 7, does the student sound like a parent giving a warning?

Performance

This is your opportunity to sit back, relax, and enjoy the performance. Encourage students to have fun while performing!

Intermission *page 16*

Assign these questions and activities for students to complete either independently or in a group.

Vocabulary Tip

For more vocabulary practice, have students discuss the following:

- Give an example of an animal that can be a predator looking for **prey.**
- Name two **species** of pets.
- Describe an **adaptation** that would help human beings run faster.

Act II Connected Readings

- **The Arctic Fox** (well below) *page 17*
- **The Anteater** (below) *page 18*
- **The Polar Bear** (on/above) *page 19*

Independent Practice
Break each Act I group into two: one group of three (with 1 well below level, 1 below, 1 on/above) and another group of three (1 well below, 1 below, 1 on/above). Assign each member a different selection based on level. Then have students read through their selections once.

Small Group Practice
Assemble the groups. As with the play rehearsals, each rehearsal in the schedule below has an activity to guide students.

1. First Rehearsal: Invite students to read aloud the titles of their selections. Have each student tell two or three things about the animal named in the title. Then ask students to read their selections aloud for the first time.

2. Vocabulary Rehearsal: Before this rehearsal, ask each student to illustrate one of the selection's vocabulary words. Give students time to share their illustrations with their groups, and invite volunteers to guess the word being represented.

3. Fluency Rehearsal: Using Expression Remind students to note the Fluency Tips for their selections. After the rehearsal, ask students to model using their tips as suggested.

4. Comprehension Rehearsal: Making Inferences Direct students to work together to answer the relevant question.

- *The Arctic Fox:* What probably happens to the fur of an Arctic fox that lives in a zoo in a warmer climate?
- *The Anteater:* If the number of insects in a tropical forest decreased sharply, what would be the effect on the anteater?
- *The Polar Bear:* Are seals safe from a polar bear? Why or why not?

5. Final Rehearsal: Observe each student's reading. Give last-minute pointers for the performance to come, modeling the pointers as appropriate.

Performance
As with the performance of the play, enjoy the reading!

Curtain Call *page 20*
Have groups answer the relevant Comprehension Prompter questions. For the Taking It Further activity, you may want to form new groups.

Fluency Tip
As a warm-up, invite each student to copy one sentence from his or her selection. Have students underline words they plan to stress when reading the sentences aloud. Then have them read the sentences to partners.

Set 6

Change Is Good

Vocabulary Write the number of a vocabulary word on the blank before its meaning.

1. gland
2. adapt
3. species
4. prey
5. camouflage
6. habitat

_____ Animal hunted and eaten by other animals

_____ Natural environment of a living thing

_____ An organ of the body that makes a special substance

_____ To disguise

_____ A group of living things that share certain characteristics

_____ To change to suit an environment or situation

Comprehension Write your answer to each question on the lines below.

1. What advantages are there to seeing animals in a zoo rather than in the wild?

_____

_____

2. Which of Uncle Mark's jokes did you think was most humorous? Why?

_____

_____

3. What is one way in which African elephants differ from Asian elephants?

_____

_____

4. Which of the animals mentioned in the play would you most like to see in the wild? Explain your choice. _____

_____

Fluency Take this page to your teacher, who will ask you to read aloud part of your Act II selection. Your teacher will record a score below.

- The student varies voice to enhance meaning.   **1   2   3   4   5**

- The student takes cues from punctuation
  for how to read the sentence.   **1   2   3   4   5**

Survivors

Overview
In this book, students will build fluency and comprehension skills by reading a **reader's theater** and the accompanying **connected readings.** The titles and leveling information appear below.

Reader's Theater
"Earthquake!" is a six-character play about four young people who are dealing with the aftermath of an earthquake.
  Timothy (well below); Sophia (well below); Narrator 1 (below); Joey (below); Julia (on/above); Narrator 2 (on/above)

Connected Readings
These three readings cover the topics of recognizing and surviving tsunamis, tornadoes, and blizzards.
  What's Going On? (1) (well below); **What's Going On? (2)** (below); **What's Going On? (3)** (on/above)

Fluency Focus
Using Punctuation

Comprehension Focus
Visualizing

Vocabulary
aftershock, durable, essentials, flustered, foresight, fragments, hunkered

Read Aloud Tip
Read the selection aloud. Next, introduce the fluency focus of **using punctuation.** Then re-read paragraph 2 of the Read Aloud, focusing on stopping at each period. Read the paragraph again. This time, ask students to listen and note how many sentences they hear by keeping a tally of the sentences on a piece of scratch paper.

Setting the Stage

Teacher Read Aloud   *pages 2–3*
This selection is about the science of fires and what to do if you are in a building that catches fire. Ask students to listen for pauses indicated by commas and dashes as you read the selection aloud.

Vocabulary   *page 4*
Use this page to introduce important vocabulary. Discuss the Word Play feature, focusing on helping students connect the words to their own background and experiences.

Fluency and Comprehension Warm-Ups   *pages 5–6*
Review these pages with students. Use the following for students who need additional help with the concepts:

- **Using Punctuation** Paying attention to punctuation helps you know how to read a selection. When you come to a dash, pause slightly longer than when you come to a comma. Study the Read Aloud to find sentences with both a dash and a comma. Choose one sentence to read aloud, pausing at each dash and comma.

- **Visualizing** Visualizing is creating pictures in your mind as you read. It means thinking about what your senses might tell you if you were part of a scene. For example, when the Read Aloud describes escaping from a burning house, think about the heat, the crackling of the fire, and the scent of smoke. Draw a picture of what you are visualizing in your mind.

21

Set 6

Act I Reader's Theater

- **Earthquake!** *pages 7–15*

Independent Practice

Set up the groups and assign each student a part. Then have students read through their assigned parts once before small group practice begins.

Small Group Practice

Assemble the groups. You may want to use the following rehearsal schedule. Each rehearsal, which should involve a complete oral read-through, has an activity to guide students.

1. First Rehearsal: Invite students to read the title and cast of characters and to look at the illustrations in the play. Ask volunteers to predict what happens to the characters. Then have students read together as a group for the first time.

2. Vocabulary Rehearsal: Have students locate and list all of the vocabulary words used in the play. Ask them to work in their groups to create a Word Web using one vocabulary word. Remind them that a Word Web can include definitions, examples, things related to the word, and so on. Provide time for groups to share their Word Webs.

3. Fluency Rehearsal: Using Punctuation During this rehearsal, encourage students to pay attention to the Fluency Tips. After the rehearsal, invite each student to choose one line with an exclamation point or an ellipsis to read aloud to the group.

4. Comprehension Rehearsal: Visualizing Guide students to focus on creating pictures in their minds as they read. After the reading, ask them to draw one scene or event they visualized. Have students share their drawings.

5. Final Rehearsal: Observe this rehearsal, focusing on students' awareness of punctuation. For example, when Julia speaks her first lines on page 7, does the student actor's voice rise at the end of each question?

Performance

This is your opportunity to sit back, relax, and enjoy the performance. Encourage students to have fun while performing!

Intermission *page 16*

Assign these questions and activities for students to complete either independently or in a group.

Vocabulary Tip

For more vocabulary practice, have students discuss the following:

- What are two things you consider **essential** at school? At home?

- If someone **hunkered** down near you, would you expect him or her to stay for a while?

- How is a **fragment** similar to a fraction?

Act II Connected Readings

- **What's Going On? (1)** (well below) *page 17*
- **What's Going On? (2)** (below) *page 18*
- **What's Going On? (3)** (on/above) *page 19*

Independent Practice

Break each Act I group into two: one group of three (with 1 well below level, 1 below, 1 on/above) and another group of three (1 well below, 1 below, 1 on/above). Assign each member a different selection based on level. Then have students read through their selections once.

Small Group Practice

Assemble the groups. As with the play rehearsals, each rehearsal in the schedule below has an activity to guide students.

1. First Rehearsal: Allow students to ponder why all three of the selections have the same title, *What's Going On?*, and to discuss their thoughts with the group. Then ask students to read their selections aloud to the group.

2. Vocabulary Rehearsal: Before this rehearsal, ask students to locate selection vocabulary words. Invite each student to choose one word to act out for other group members to guess.

3. Fluency Rehearsal: Using Punctuation Focus students' attention on watching for punctuation cues by reviewing the fluency instruction on page 5. Then have students read aloud paragraph 1 of their selections, using punctuation cues.

4. Comprehension Rehearsal: Visualizing Guide students to focus on visualizing as they read. After the reading, ask each student to draw one visualized scene or event. Have students share their drawings.

5. Final Rehearsal: Observe each student's reading. Give last-minute pointers for the performance to come, modeling the pointers as appropriate.

Performance

As with the performance of the play, enjoy the reading!

Curtain Call *page 20*

Have groups answer the relevant Comprehension Prompter questions. For the Taking It Further activity, you may want to form new groups.

Fluency Tip

Before the performance, remind students that a period is a signal to stop reading. Then have each student choose a paragraph from his or her selection to read aloud to the group. As group members listen, ask them to keep tallies of how many times they hear the reader stop reading. Allow students to compare their tallies to see if they come up with the same number of sentences read by the reader.

23

Set 6

Survivors

Vocabulary Finish the story by writing a vocabulary word on each blank.

hunkered	flustered	fragments	essentials
durable	foresight	aftershock	

Gloria searched through her backpack. "I put my sunglasses in here—along with other **(1)** _____, like sunscreen and bottled water," she said. "I had the **(2)** _____ to know I'd need them on the hike."

"Oh, no!" she exclaimed, holding up two **(3)** _____ of plastic. "I guess cheap sunglasses aren't very **(4)** _____."

"Don't get **(5)** _____," said Tony. "I have an extra pair you can borrow."

Comprehension Write your answer to each question on the lines below.

1. Why does Julia tell Timothy to be careful when he goes into the bedrooms?

_____

2. Where would you go for help if disaster struck and you were home alone?

_____

3. What do you think the teens and their parents learned from their experience?

_____

_____

4. What is one thing you predict Julia's parents will do to make their home more earthquake-proof? _____

_____

Fluency Take this page to your teacher, who will ask you to read aloud part of your Act II selection. Your teacher will record a score below.

- The student reads smoothly, with few stumbles.   **1   2   3   4   5**
- The student takes cues from punctuation, pausing and stopping naturally.   **1   2   3   4   5**

Dig It!

Overview
In this book, students will build fluency and comprehension skills by reading a **reader's theater** and the accompanying **connected readings.** The titles and leveling information appear below.

Reader's Theater
"The Vacation" is a six-character play about a family who makes a fantastic discovery while working on an archaeological dig.
   Jonathan (well below); Carla (well below); Dad (below); Narrator (below); Mom (on/above); Jessie (on/above)

Connected Readings
These three readings cover the topics of the ruins of Pompeii, a dinosaur discovery, and prehistoric artifacts found in Laos.
   Pompeii (well below); **Jane** (below); **The Plain of Jars** (on/above)

Fluency Focus
Using Punctuation

Comprehension Focus
Making Connections

Vocabulary
archaeologists, artifact, dig, fossil, prehistoric, trowel, unit

Read Aloud Tip
After reading the selection once, introduce the fluency focus of **using punctuation.** Then point out that a comma indicates a pause. Direct students' attention to paragraph 1 of the Read Aloud. Ask for volunteers to read aloud any sentences that include commas.

Setting the Stage

Teacher Read Aloud *pages 2–3*
This selection is about Ötzi, the prehistoric man whose well-preserved body was found in the mountains of Europe five millenniums after his death. Read the selection aloud, modeling good fluency. At the end of each paragraph, stop and re-read one sentence, asking students to read along with you.

Vocabulary *page 4*
Use this page to introduce important vocabulary. Discuss the Word Play feature, reminding students to use the supplied definitions to help with their responses.

Fluency and Comprehension Warm-Ups *pages 5–6*
Review these pages with students. Use the following for students who need additional help with the concepts:

- **Using Punctuation** Ending punctuation gives you clues for reading sentences. Stop when you come to the end of a sentence with a period. Raise your voice when a sentence ends with an exclamation point. Practice these techniques as you read paragraph 3 of the Read Aloud.

- **Making Connections** When you make connections, you ask yourself what you already know about a topic or how it connects to something you have read or heard earlier. Think about the Read Aloud. What do you know about prehistoric people or animals that helps you understand this text?

25

Set 6

Act I Reader's Theater

• The Vacation *pages 7–15*

Independent Practice

Set up the groups and assign each student a part. Then have students read through their assigned parts once before small group practice begins.

Small Group Practice

Assemble the groups. You may want to use the following rehearsal schedule. Each rehearsal, which should involve a complete oral read-through, has an activity to guide students.

1. First Rehearsal: Guide students through a play preview by reading the title, character list, and stage directions and by viewing the illustrations. Invite volunteers to make some predictions about what might happen in the play. Then invite students to read together as a group.

2. Vocabulary Rehearsal: Direct students to locate and list the vocabulary words used in the play. Then have students work together to find and discuss two vocabulary words that are related in some way. For example, students could discuss how *archaeologists* work on *digs*.

3. Fluency Rehearsal: Using Punctuation During this rehearsal, encourage students to note question marks and exclamation points in their lines and to read these lines in a questioning voice or an excited one, as appropriate. After the rehearsal, invite students to choose one question or exclamation to read aloud to the group.

4. Comprehension Rehearsal: Making Connections Ask students to think about connections they can make between this play and their own experiences. Then have them answer the questions below.

- How does this play remind you of other plays or stories you have read?
- How does the way members of this family interact remind you of other people you know?

5. Final Rehearsal: Observe this rehearsal, focusing on students' awareness of punctuation. For example, on page 7, does the student reading Carla's lines use the capital letters as a clue to stress the word *SOMEPLACE?*

Performance

This is your opportunity to sit back, relax, and enjoy the performance. Encourage students to have fun while performing!

Intermission *page 16*

Assign these questions and activities for students to complete either independently or in a group.

Vocabulary Tip

For more vocabulary practice, have students discuss the following:

- Other than an **archaeologist,** who might consider a **trowel** a useful tool?

- What is one thing **archaeologists** can learn from **fossils?**

- Why is studying **artifacts** one of the few ways we have to learn about **prehistoric** people?

Act II Connected Readings

- **Pompeii** (well below) *page 17*
- **Jane** (below) *page 18*
- **The Plain of Jars** (on/above) *page 19*

Independent Practice

Break each Act I group into two: one group of three (with 1 well below level, 1 below, 1 on/above) and another group of three (1 well below, 1 below, 1 on/above). Assign each member a different selection based on level. Then have students read through their selections once.

Small Group Practice

Assemble the groups. As with the play rehearsals, each rehearsal in the schedule below has an activity to guide students.

1. First Rehearsal: Have students preview their selections, noting any proper nouns that name places. Let them practice reading these place names to a partner and locating each place on a world map. Then ask students to read their selections aloud to the group.

2. Vocabulary Rehearsal: Before this rehearsal, ask each student to illustrate one vocabulary word from his or her selection. Then have students read their selections aloud. After reading, ask students to share their illustrations, and have the others guess each word illustrated.

3. Fluency Rehearsal: Using Punctuation Review page 5. Then have students read aloud the Fluency Tips for their selections. Remind them to apply the tips as they read. After the rehearsal, you may want to have each student read aloud a sentence or paragraph, demonstrating to others in the group how to apply the tip.

> ### Fluency Tip
> As a warm-up, invite students to find and practice reading aloud a line from their selection that includes a comma or a dash. Remind them to pause slightly longer for the dash than they do for the comma.

4. Comprehension Rehearsal: Making Connections Ask students to write two sentences that explain how their selection connects to the play or to the Read Aloud.

5. Final Rehearsal: Observe each student's reading. Give last-minute pointers for the performance to come, modeling the pointers as appropriate.

Performance

As with the performance of the play, enjoy the reading!

Curtain Call *page 20*

Have groups answer the relevant Comprehension Prompter questions. For the Taking It Further activity, you may want to form new groups.

Set 6

Dig It!

Vocabulary Write each vocabulary word on the blank where it belongs.

| dig | fossils | artifacts | prehistoric |
| trowels | archaeologists | units | |

1. We used _____ to put soil in the pots.
2. The workers uncovered an ancient tomb at a(n) _____ in Egypt.
3. This museum has many dinosaur _____ on display.
4. In _____ times, hunters killed such animals as woolly mammoths.
5. The _____ need to be patient and careful as they do their jobs.

Comprehension Write your answer to each question on the lines below.

1. Which character in the play reminds you the most of yourself? How are you like this character? _____

   _____

2. Why is it important to remove the soil slowly and carefully when working on a dig? _____

   _____

3. What do you think you would like most about being an archaeologist? What would you like least? _____

   _____

4. How do Carla's feelings change from the beginning of the play to the end?

   _____

   _____

Fluency Take this page to your teacher, who will ask you to read aloud part of your Act II selection. Your teacher will record a score below.

- The student reads smoothly, with few stumbles.   **1   2   3   4   5**
- The student takes cues from punctuation, pausing and stopping naturally.   **1   2   3   4   5**

Fight for the Right

Overview
In this book, students will build fluency and comprehension skills by reading a **reader's theater** and the accompanying **connected readings.** The titles and leveling information appear below.

Reader's Theater
"Sojourner Truth" is a six-character play about students who are working on a project about Sojourner Truth, a former slave who inspired many abolitionists.
> Narrator (well below); Hidori (well below); Kendi (below); Sojourner (below); Berto (on/above); Ines (on/above)

Connected Readings
These three readings cover the topics of social reformers Evangeline Booth, Lewis Hine, and Jane Addams.
> **Evangeline Booth** (well below); **Lewis Hine** (below); **Jane Addams** (on/above)

Fluency Focus
Reading with Word Accuracy

Comprehension Focus
Summarizing

Vocabulary
antislavery, auction, autobiography, convention, involved, passion, sue

Read Aloud Tip
Introduce the fluency focus of **reading with word accuracy.** Write *reformers* and *abolitionists* on the board. Point out that good readers think about how to pronounce difficult words before they read aloud. They look at each word part and then put the parts together. Have students read each word with you, first stressing the separate syllables and then reading each whole word aloud.

Setting the Stage

Teacher Read Aloud   *pages 2–3*
This selection is about social reform in the United States and some of the individuals who fought injustice. Ask students to listen carefully as you read the selection aloud.

Vocabulary   *page 4*
Use this page to introduce important vocabulary. Discuss the Word Play feature, focusing on helping students connect the words to their own background and experience.

Fluency and Comprehension Warm-Ups   *pages 5–6*
Review these pages with students. Use the following for students who need additional help with the concepts:

- **Reading with Word Accuracy** When you come to unfamiliar words, remember to look for parts of the word that you know. Put the parts together to say a word that makes sense. Then practice saying the word. Try doing this with words from the Read Aloud, such as *petitions* and *salvation*.

- **Summarizing** Summarizing is retelling the important parts of what you read. Look at paragraph 4 of the Read Aloud. Name two or three of the most important ideas in the paragraph. Put those ideas together in a one-sentence summary of the paragraph.

29

Set 6

Act I Reader's Theater

- **Sojourner Truth** *pages 7–15*

Independent Practice
Set up the groups and assign each student a part. Then have students read through their assigned parts once before small group practice begins.

Small Group Practice
Assemble the groups. You may want to use the following rehearsal schedule. Each rehearsal, which should involve a complete oral read-through, has an activity to guide students.

1. First Rehearsal: Invite students to scan the entire play to find italicized stage directions. Remind students that these directions tell actors how to speak or what to do. Discuss the reason for having the narrator and Sojourner sit separately from the other actors. Then ask students to read together as a group for the first time.

2. Vocabulary Rehearsal: Have students locate the vocabulary words used in the play and write each word on a separate index card. Then have students take turns choosing a card, reading the word aloud, and using the word in a sentence.

3. Fluency Rehearsal: Reading with Word Accuracy Before this rehearsal, review the fluency instruction on page 5. Remind students to pay attention to the Fluency Tips as they read. Then, after the rehearsal, ask each student to choose one tip and apply it to an example from the play. For example, the tip on page 8 could be used with the names *Ulster* and *Isabella* on that page.

4. Comprehension Rehearsal: Summarizing After this rehearsal, have students work together in groups to complete a Story Map that identifies important events in Sojourner Truth's life. Remind students that the Story Map should include just facts. It should not include details. Then challenge groups to use the Story Map as a guide for writing a four- or five-sentence biographical sketch of Sojourner.

5. Final Rehearsal: Observe this rehearsal, focusing on students' ability to read with word accuracy. For example, do actors look for word parts they recognize to accurately read names, such as *Van Wagener* and *Dumont?*

Performance
This is your opportunity to sit back, relax, and enjoy the performance. Encourage students to have fun while performing!

Intermission   *page 16*
Assign these questions and activities for students to complete either independently or in a group.

Vocabulary Tip
For more vocabulary practice, have students discuss the following:

- If you sit on the sidelines at a sports event, how can you still be **involved** in the game?

- What are some reasons people **sue** individuals or companies?

- Name another word that includes the prefix *anti-*, as in **antislavery.** What does the word mean?

Act II Connected Readings

- **Evangeline Booth** (well below) *page 17*
- **Lewis Hine** (below) *page 18* • **Jane Addams** (on/above) *page 19*

Independent Practice

Break each Act I group into two: one group of three (with 1 well below level, 1 below, 1 on/above) and another group of three (1 well below, 1 below, 1 on/above). Assign each member a different selection based on level. Then have students read through their selections once.

Small Group Practice

Assemble the groups. As with the play rehearsals, each rehearsal in the schedule below has an activity to guide students.

1. First Rehearsal: Invite students to read aloud the titles of their selections. Allow volunteers to share any information they know about the people whose names are in the titles. Then ask students to read aloud in groups for the first time.

2. Vocabulary Rehearsal: Before this rehearsal, ask students to locate any selection vocabulary words. Have each student use a sheet of paper to complete the applicable sentence starter below. Allow students to share their sentences.

- *Evangeline Booth:* I have a **passion** for _____.
- *Lewis Hine:* I would like to be more **involved** in _____.
- *Jane Addams:* One thing I would include in my **autobiography** is _____.

3. Fluency Rehearsal: Reading with Word Accuracy After the reading, challenge each student to choose a multipart word from his or her selection. Invite the student to read the word aloud, slowly saying the individual parts first and then blending to say the word naturally.

4. Comprehension Rehearsal: Summarizing Direct students to create posters that summarize what they learned about the individuals featured in the selections. Have each student write the person's name at the top of a sheet of construction paper and then add three facts about the person. Invite them to add an illustration.

5. Final Rehearsal: Observe each student's reading. Give last-minute pointers for the performance to come, modeling the pointers as appropriate.

Performance

As with the performance of the play, enjoy the reading!

Curtain Call   *page 20*

Have groups answer the relevant Comprehension Prompter questions. For the Taking It Further activity, you may want to form new groups.

Fluency Tip

Before the first rehearsal, write the names of the three individuals featured in the selections on the board. As appropriate, draw lines to show the word parts in each name. Invite volunteers to say the parts of a name and then blend the parts together.

Set 6

Fight for the Right

Vocabulary Write the vocabulary word that answers each question.

passion	convention	auction	sue
involved	antislavery	autobiography	

1. Which word names a way to sell something? _____
2. In what movement would an abolitionist participate? _____
3. What would you call an account you write about your own life? _____
4. Which word describes an intense feeling? _____
5. Which word describes a large meeting? _____

Comprehension Write your answer to each question on the lines below.

1. What do you admire most about Sojourner Truth? _____
   _____
2. What was the most surprising or interesting thing you learned from reading this play? _____
3. What are two ways in which your life would be different if you couldn't read and write? _____
   _____
4. Why do you think Sojourner was able to influence people to join the fight against slavery? _____
   _____

Fluency Take this page to your teacher, who will ask you to read aloud part of your Act II selection. Your teacher will record a score below.

- The student reads all words accurately, self-correcting if necessary.   1 2 3 4 5
- The student blends together parts of a word.   1 2 3 4 5

Answer Key

It's Greek to Me!

Act I Vocabulary Tip (Suggested responses for 1 and 2)
"Innocent until proven guilty" means you cannot assume a person is guilty just because he or she has been accused of a crime./A vain person would spend a lot of time looking in the mirror, fixing his or her hair, and so on./Responses will vary.

Act II Comprehension Rehearsal (Suggested responses)
Liar: "You cannot believe . . ."/brimming: "Goodness is everywhere."/prowess: ". . . intense strength . . ."

BLM: Vocabulary
1. innocent; 2. destiny; 3. deceiving; 4. mortal; 5. maiden

BLM: Comprehension (Suggested responses for 1 and 2)
1. Aphrodite sent Eros away, so no one fell in love. People fought instead./2. He wanted Psyche to love him for himself, not because he was a god./3. Responses will vary./4. Responses will vary.

From the Inside Out

Act I Vocabulary Tip (Suggested responses)
Height, hair color, eye color, skin color, intelligence, and so on are due to heredity./You would be shorter than normal./Nutrients from digested food travel through the body in the bloodstream.

BLM: Vocabulary
Answers from top to bottom should read as follows: 2, 4, 7, 1, 3, 5, 6

BLM: Comprehension (Suggested responses)
1. Daniel is concerned that he is too short./2. Pete Pituitary./3. The endocrine system consists of a group of glands that work with your bloodstream. They control your energy, your responses to the world, and your growth./4. Daniel learns that he is developing normally and that he just grows at a different rate than some of his friends do.

Secrets in Stone

Act I Vocabulary Tip (Suggested responses)
An archaeologist looks for artifacts that tell how people lived. A geologist looks for rocks that tell about the history of the earth./A paleontologist.

Act II Comprehension Rehearsal (Suggested response)
Easter Island: Archaeologists do not know why people long ago erected huge stone statues on Easter Island./Rosetta Stone: Ancient writing carved on the Rosetta Stone has helped people figure out how to read hieroglyphics./Stonehenge: The United Kingdom's Stonehenge is a circle of large stones that archaeologists believe was used as an ancient gathering place.

BLM: Vocabulary
1. decipher; 2. geologist; 3. replica; 4. paleontologist; 5. hieroglyphics

BLM: Comprehension (Suggested responses for 1–3)
1. Ancient people carved pictures into stones to tell stories and to record historical events./2. The stones are unique and should stay on Easter Island./Many museums can display replicas at the same time so more people can see what the stones are like./3. Discovering the Rosetta Stone helped people figure out what hieroglyphic symbols mean./4. Responses will vary.

Who's Your Mummy?

Act I Vocabulary Tip (Suggested response for 2)
Responses will vary./A tomb holds a body or bodies. A gravestone marks where a body is buried./Responses will vary.

BLM: Vocabulary
1. archaeologist; 2. vile; 3. mummy; 4. tomb; 5. balcony

BLM: Comprehension (Suggested responses for 1, 3, and 4)
1. Jenna doesn't want to go to Egypt or go into a tomb, but her brothers were excited about it./2. Responses will vary./3. New discoveries in tombs are interesting to people./4. The author wants readers to wonder whether the tomb really is cursed.

Set 6

Answer Key

Change Is Good

Act I Comprehension Rehearsal (Suggested responses)
Giraffes thousands of years ago were probably different because the climate was different. They might have had shorter necks because the trees were shorter then./The author wants you to learn that animals have many interesting and unique characteristics.

Act I Vocabulary Tip (Suggested responses for 1 and 3)
A praying mantis catches and eats other insects./ Responses will vary./Longer legs would let human beings cover more ground faster.

Act II Comprehension Rehearsal (Suggested responses)
The Arctic Fox: The fox's fur is probably not as thick./The Anteater: The anteater would starve to death or would start eating something else./The Polar Bear: Seals aren't safe because, even when they are in the water or under the ice, polar bears can smell them.

BLM: Vocabulary
Answers from top to bottom should read as follows: 4, 6, 1, 5, 3, 2

BLM: Comprehension (Suggested responses for 1 and 3)
1. You can get close to animals that would be too dangerous to approach in the wild./2. Responses will vary./3. Female African elephants have tusks, but female Asian elephants do not./4. Responses will vary.

Survivors

Act I Vocabulary Tip (Suggested responses)
At school: books and paper are essential. At home: food and a bed are essential./You would expect the person to stay for a while, because hunkered means "settled in for a period of time."/A fragment and a fraction can both be parts of a whole thing.

BLM: Vocabulary
1. essentials; 2. foresight; 3. fragments; 4. durable; 5. flustered

BLM: Comprehension (Suggested responses for 1, 3, and 4)
1. Furniture could be leaning and could fall on him./2. Responses will vary./3. They learned that it is important to know what to do in the case of a disaster./4. They will bolt heavy furniture to the walls.

Dig It!

Act I Vocabulary Tip (Suggested responses)
A gardener might use a trowel./Archaeologists can learn how big a plant or animal was./Prehistoric people didn't leave any written record of how they lived.

BLM: Vocabulary
1. trowels; 2. dig; 3. fossils; 4. prehistoric; 5. archaeologists

BLM: Comprehension (Suggested responses for 2 and 4)
1. Responses will vary./2. Artifacts are very fragile; working quickly might destroy them./3. Responses will vary./4. At first, Carla didn't want to go on the dig. After the family's discovery, she wanted to go on another dig.

Answer Key

Fight for the Right

Act I Vocabulary Tip (Suggested responses)
You could cheer for the players or keep track of the score./People sometimes sue drivers who cause accidents or doctors who make mistakes./The word *antiwar* means "against war."

BLM: Vocabulary
1. auction; 2. antislavery; 3. autobiography;
4. passion; 5. convention

BLM: Comprehension (Suggested response for 4)
1. Responses will vary./2. Responses will vary./
3. Responses will vary./4. Hearing about what happened to Sojourner made listeners realize that slaves were real people who were treated cruelly and unjustly.